Coraleigh Parker

HANGING
KOKEDAMA

Creating Potless Plants for the Home

Coraleigh Parker

HANGING
KOKEDAMA

Creating Potless Plants for the Home

Design and layout copyright
© 2018 Quarto Publishing Group plc
Text copyright © Coraleigh Parker
Specially commissioned photography
© 2018 Larnie Nicolson

Front cover image features Cole and Son 'Woods' wallpaper

First published in 2018 by
Jacqui Small, an imprint of The Quarto Group
The Old Brewery, 6 Blundell Street,
London N7 9BH, United Kingdom
T (0)20 7700 6700 F (0)20 7700 8066
www.QuartoKnows.com

Publisher: Jacqui Small
Senior Commissioning Editor/Project Editor: Eszter Karpati
Managing Editor: Emma Heyworth-Dunn
Designer: Caroline Clark
Production: Maeve Healy

ISBN: 978-1-911127-39-0

A catalogue record for this book
is available from the British Library.

2020 2019 2018
10 9 8 7 6 5 4 3 2 1

Printed in China

MIX
Paper from
responsible sources
FSC® C008047

AUGUST 2018

CONTENTS

Jacqui
Small

WHAT IS KOKEDAMA?

A variant of bonsai, kokedama is the Japanese art of creating potless plants using a unique soil mixture, moss and string.

苔 Koke = moss
玉 Tama = ball

There is something intrinsically inviting and soothing about the form of kokedama, through the juxtaposition of its controlled and wild aspects. It is a manifestation of wabi-sabi, or the Japanese art of finding beauty in imperfection. All the elements which keep bonsai from falling into obscurity are also present in kokedama, but in a much more accessible format.

Economical design, which seeks to use a minimum of components, along with displaying natural processes and naturally occurring objects, is becoming increasingly mainstream. As more people choose to see the beauty in the roughness of nature, the room in their lives for meaningless clutter diminishes.

As a hobby, the art of making kokedama is as rewarding as it gets. The act of putting our hands in direct contact with natural materials literally grounds us.

The wrapping process is very meditative; the action requires bilateral coordination – that is, to use both hands simultaneously and independently. And because both hands are required to wrap, and each must perform separate and independent actions, it is very difficult to think about anything else. One becomes completely present in the moment.

Additionally, when creating the heavily wrapped style, there is also a meditative quality to the repetitive but nuanced action of wrapping string around a sphere. It is almost hypnotic.

Many amateur kokedama artists use the art as a way to unwind after hectic days at work, or frenetically busy periods in their lives. The action of making a kokedama

Opposite: Jack the dog ponders over a suspended *Oxalis triangularis*

provides a small haven of tranquillity and peace that centres one's energy back into the body and self.

Kokedama evolved from the nearai style of bonsai, which has exposed roots as part of the aesthetic. Normally they are grown in a pot for such a long period of time that their roots completely fill the pot and they can be removed and displayed without harming the tree. To stop the roots from drying during the transformation or root ageing process, moss is placed over the roots to cover and protect them.

The traditional form of kokedama is created using a mixture of peat and akadama soil turned into a sphere. This is split and hollowed out in the centre. A small plant with its roots wrapped in sphagnum moss is inserted and the 2 halves are joined again. Sometimes the outside is seeded with grass, or wrapped with wild woolly moss.

The more modern method is to leave out the clay-based akadama soil altogether. The best style to learn with is to simply wrap the roots and soil in a thick layer of sphagnum moss. This provides a container to hold in the moisture and reduce the amount of watering needed. The moss is like a dense sponge; it holds the water and releases it slowly back to the roots. It also prevents evaporation of moisture from the soil, as would normally occur with a pot.

The main difference though between a pot and a kokedama is the way the roots respond. Roots essentially adhere to one type of behaviour, which is to seek water. The root activity is binary: as a very general rule, if there is water, they grow – if there isn't, they don't. (This is a topic that some scientists dedicate years to, so take with a pinch of salt.) What this means in a pot is that the roots always encounter water so they continue to grow. They grow and grow, around and around the inside of the pot until they exclude any moisture or nutrients from entering.

In a kokedama, however, the roots which come to the outside of the ball encounter air. If the air is dry, the roots stop growing. Instead of using long fat roots to explore for water, the plant grows many fine roots within the ball.

With some plants, such as trees, the size of the canopy is determined by the size of the root mass. As this is defined by the size of the ball, trees will stay as small examples of their larger wild counterparts.

You will probably gain more pleasure from your kokedama, and observe their needs best, if you assume that plants are people too: try to love them like you would a friend, or a pet. Get to know your plants. Don't expect them to give you something for nothing. All relationships are about give and take. When you give your plants the attention they need, they will happily reciprocate by giving you beautiful green goodness to look upon. They will gladly fill your life with tranquillity and peace.

Opposite: Syngonium podophyllum hanging out in the kitchen

Curating kokedama

Kokedama are perfect for completing a space because they are so versatile. They can be made in any size, shape or colour to suit the setting.

Suspended kokedama add depth and texture to spaces and displays. Because they are suspended, it is easy to adjust their final position and height to maximize the effect.

They are strongly rooted in the wabi-sabi philosophy so it is always a matter of "less is more". Don't over-style kokedama by cluttering too many objects around them. Use them as you would a beautiful painting or artwork.

Use green plants with green-covered kokedama to add lushness to a stark corner and to soften a room. Use small and delicate kokedama where they can be appreciated at closer proximity and where they won't become lost or obscured by too many other objects.

Choose large lush green leaves for backgrounds of soft texture to add drama.

Use delicate structural branches and leaves against large blank backgrounds to draw the eye to the detail. Use the height of the kokedama to focus the eye where you want it to go.

Combine finely detailed plants with large monocolour objects for contrast and visual drama.

Be careful when hanging against walls as the moisture from the ball can cause damage. If the surface is porous, there will be a risk of mould and mildew developing where the kokedama is touching it. Be sure to use a hook or hanger which protrudes out from the wall enough to avoid contact.

Make sure that the light is right for the plant; many plants used indoors prefer not to have sun touch them directly on their foliage or flowers. That is not to say they like darkness; most in fact need good, bright light. You can achieve this by hanging them so their foliage sits above or beyond the limit of the sun's rays penetrating into the room.

Opposite: Clustering a group of cacti kokedama into a single display adds impact *Overleaf:* Coco the dog lounges comfortably beneath two cyclamen, an oxalis and a colocasia

HOW TO MAKE KOKEDAMA

Kokedama are, once mastered, very easy and rewarding to make. It is such a great art form to take up as a hobby, combining the truly grounding practice of getting one's hands dirty with the artistic gratification of creating a beautiful object.

When contemplating what to create it is easy to become overwhelmed or overexcited by the potential choices in front of you, but remember to start small and build up your confidence. When learning, it is best to start with a size that fits easily into your hands. Try doing easy-care, small plants such as succulents to begin with; once you get the hang of it, move onto creating bigger or more challenging plants.

The most important thing to consider is where your kokedama will be living. This will inform your plant choice. Some plants, such as cacti, prefer hot, sunny rooms while others, such as ferns, are happy in low light and cooler temperatures.

The type of plant you choose will also inform your choice of wrapping material. There is the aesthetic to consider but also the lifespan of your chosen wrapping fibre. Natural fibres will break down over time and may need to be replaced or removed. Take this into account when designing your kokedama. Try sketching out different rooms and adding kokedama to the picture to see how it feels. Sketch different plants as kokedama to see what the final effect will be.

Making kokedama is messy. The moss requires soaking and subsequently will create puddles and drips. The soil recipes require various ingredients to be measured and mixed. Although it is not strictly an outside activity, one must be prepared. Set up a designated area with all the required items. It is not necessary to wear gloves, and many find that wearing them inhibits one's ability to wrap and manage the ball. Sticking to organic ingredients will limit exposure to harmful substances. The beauty of making kokedama is the contact with the natural ingredients.

Opposite: Echeveria elegans bathing in the afternoon light

Tools for the job

Making kokedama is a simple enough task; having everything you need at your fingertips will ensure a smooth and pleasurable experience which you will look forward to each time.

GETTING STARTED

Space to make a mess

Have a space which can handle the drips and drops, or create one with a dust sheet (drop cloth) or paper. If your table is not waterproof, cover it with plastic or waxed paper.

Spoon and bowl to mix and measure soil

Allocate a bowl and spoon specifically for working with soil and things planty, and keep them separate from those used for

Left, clockwise from top left: Measuring spoon, cloth, good scissors, brush and dustpan (shovel), mister, nail brush, secateurs *Opposite, left and right:* Strings, hooks and chains for a variety of wrapping and hanging styles

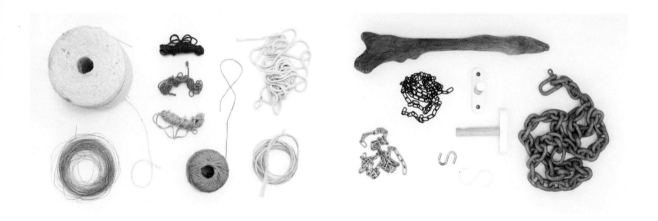

eating. The bowl will need to be large enough to accommodate the recipes you intend to make.

Cloth to wipe down surfaces

Because you are dealing with soil ingredients, allocate a cloth specifically for kokedama clean down. Keep it separate from food prep cloths.

Scissors to cut string

The ideal scissors are sharp and sturdy.

Brush and dustpan (shovel) to sweep up after

There will inevitably be mess even if you are super careful.

Nail brush to clean away the evidence of your foray into nature

Although it is a sacred right to participate in and interact with nature, for some reason it is not acceptable to appear in respectable society with evidence of such activities under one's nails.

Mister to clean off plant leaves

Once your kokedama is complete, there will be bits and pieces on his leaves and ball.

Secateurs to prune and shape

Sharp secateurs are essential for clean and accurate pruning of plants. Using blunt or dirty blades can create a ragged wound on a plant which can provide access for disease or infection.

WRAPPING OPTIONS

The type of string will relate to the type of plant you select, or vice versa. Natural fibre will degrade over time. The contact with moisture will cause decomposition. With some plants, the rate at which the string deteriorates is close enough to the rate at which the roots of the plants grow so by the time the string rots away, the ball will hold itself together with its own roots. Plants that stay wet, such as ferns, will need synthetic wrapping which doesn't degrade, as the constant contact with water will cause natural fibres to deteriorate very quickly. It doesn't need to be the only wrapping; you can use nylon first and then cover with natural twine to achieve the desired aesthetic. Or if you want a more industrial feel, use a soft wire to hold the ball together.

HANGING OPTIONS

Hanging options are truly only limited by your imagination. The easiest thing is to affix a hook to a wall or ceiling to suspend from. Affix 2 hooks to a wall and string a chain between them, then hang kokedama along the length of chain. Affix a hook to a sunny wall and suspend a branch from which to hang kokedama. Suspend a pole or bar across a window and use this to display various kokedama using "S" hooks or loops of twine or wire. The pole system allows for easy access for watering. Make a loop around the ball of the kokedama, or tie string to 3 sides. Alternatively slip a hook under the twine of the wrapping. Very small "S" hooks used for hanging curtains are a great way to hang kokedama from small chains without detracting from the silhouette.

Soil ingredients

This is by far the most important part of making kokedama; it's one thing to wrap up a plant in moss, it's another thing entirely to create a home for a plant friend which he will be happy to live in for years to come.

Sphagnum moss

A thick layer of sphagnum is critical to keeping the soil and roots inside happy. If you only apply a thin layer, the moisture will evaporate rapidly from the soil, much more so than if the plant was in a pot, and you will find yourself watering constantly. This is draining for you and stressful for the plant to be dry, then wet, then dry again in rapid succession.

Coconut husk chips

Made from shredded coconut husks, this mulch is a by-product of the coconut oil industry so the energy in creating it is already reduced. It is also very porous and holds its structure for a long time. Use it for plants that need space and air around their roots and prefer humidity over liquid moisture, such as epiphytes.

Coconut fibre

This is extracted from between the outer husk and hard internal shell of the coconut. For some plants that don't require frequent watering or dislike fluctuating moisture levels, an extra layer outside the moss can help hold humidity within the ball without inhibiting airflow. Available as loose fibres or mats.

Coir

Coir dust, left over from extracting coconut fibre, is processed into blocks and used as an alternative to moss peat. Coir retains and releases water slowly, making it ideal for plants that like damp conditions; it's a buffer in the watering schedule.

Compost

Many plants rely on organic matter decomposition and all the natural activity of that process. As a booster, especially for trees, fruit and flowers, add compost to commercial potting mixes. This only serves for the first year, after which they will need a liquid fertilizer.

Water crystals

Highly absorbent crystals hold more than 100 times their weight in water. These little beauties act as tiny water reserves within the ball. Soak them first before adding them to your soil mixture.

Perlite

Some plants don't like constant access to water and prefer to dry out almost completely between watering. Perlite is a porous neutral substrate which doesn't hold water. It allows the soil to drain by moving the water downwards and creating little pockets of air.

Organic slow-release fertilizer

This helps your plant feel that the kokedama is a good place to live. If there's a steady source of moisture and food, he will happily grow roots inside the ball without striving for other nutrients. Subsequent feeding will be required.

Opposite, clockwise from top left: Coconut fibre, dried sphagnum moss, coconut chips, perlite, coir (from ground coconut husk), compost, fertilizer, water retention crystals

Wrapping

Assemble all the things you will need for the project. Make sure you have a space which is either mess-proofed or easily cleaned.

Laying a dust sheet (drop cloth) down under a table where you will be working is an easy way to contain loose bits and pieces.

Thickness of moss

It is very important to make a layer of moss around the roots which is thick enough to provide protection from evaporation. If the layer is too thin, the moss will suck the moisture from the soil as its surface dries. A thick layer of moss will provide a barrier and contain the moisture within. There is no such thing as too much moss.

Wrapping styles

The most popular style of wrapping for learning is "evenly random". This technique requires that string is coiled consistently over the entire surface of the ball, but not in any particular pattern. There are many variations on wrapping, limited only by your imagination. An easy one to try is the 2–7 technique. For this technique imagine a clock face on your kokedama. Start at position 2 o'clock and then wind towards 7 o'clock. Rotate the ball a fraction and repeat. This results in a symmetrical pattern.

Left: Cyclamen wrapped using soaked, dry sphagnum and tied with flax fibre parcel twine

1. Remove plant from his pot and carefully loosen his roots. Try not to cause too much damage as many plants are susceptible to root shock from over-handling of their roots.

2. Empty saturated moss onto a work surface (counter) and form into a disk (like a big meat patty). Press the moss with flat hands to compress into a pancake. **TIP:** Water will squeeze out so be prepared for the mess.

3. Place the plant and soil onto the moss pancake. **TIP:** Try to keep both plant and soil in the centre of the flattened moss.

4. Mix up the appropriate soil recipe for your chosen plant. Add the new mixture of soil to the plant. **TIP:** If you have soil mixture left over, keep it in an airtight container to use next time.

5. Slide your hands underneath the pancake on both sides of the plant and lift up like a taco to cover the root ball. Gather in the remaining moss to completely cover the root ball and soil.

6. Compress the moss into a covering all around the plant. **TIP:** Don't be shy, you can squish it fairly firmly without damaging the plant. The firmer you get the moss now, the easier the next part will be.

7. Tie a belt around the centre of your ball with one end of your string. Make a knot so you have an anchor to start twining from. **TIP:** Tie this as tight as you can without chopping the ball in half. Don't hold back.

8. Tilt the ball up carefully so you can loop all the way over and under. **TIP:** These don't need to look pretty; they are just to hold it all together.

9. Coil the string around the ball in an evenly random pattern. **TIP:** Keep a firm pressure on the string; try to compress the moss as you wrap. **TIP:** Use the edge of the table so the leaves don't get crushed.

10. Press down firmly and roll the ball back and forth to make it round. Pat down to shape it all over. **TIP:** Do this before you finish or you may end up with saggy string. **TIP:** Add more string to keep in shape.

11. Poke the end of the string back into the ball with the closed scissors. **TIP:** Tuck the string into the ball in an opposite direction to secure it.

12. Trim any hairy bits sticking out from the ball, or any stray moss.

Sheet moss

If you fancy your creation in verdant green, and instantly so, then this quick cheat is for you! Lush green sheet moss will grow over time to cover kokedama which are left outside. If leaving your kokedama outside is not practical, or you want the look straight away, then read on.

Once you have made your kokedama, it is possible to attach green moss to the outside.

You will need a large piece of sheet moss, either collected from the wild (with landowner's permission), or purchased from a moss supplier or florist. The piece will need to be large enough to cover the whole ball. If one large piece isn't available then several smaller pieces will work, but it will be slightly more challenging.

The main thing to remember is wherever you source your moss from, you will need to be able to replicate its growing conditions to a certain degree. In general moss requires cool temperatures, high humidity, and protection from draughts. Moss is highly sensitive to heat and will get scorched very easily. If you collect wild moss from a crisp and damp environment and subsequently put it next to your lovely warm hearth, it will probably be less than impressed to say the least.

It will also want to be in contact as much as possible with whatever surface it is on. So make sure it is stuck on nice and tight. If air can get underneath the moss, it will dry out and lose its lush green hue.

Right: Maidenhair fern kokedama covered with live sheet moss

1. Lie your kokedama on his side and place the biggest piece of sheet moss over the top side.

2a. Apply enough staples to the outside edges to hold the moss in place.

2b. Alternatively, tie on enough nylon fishing line to hold the moss firmly onto the ball.

3. Continue to add and attach pieces of sheet moss until your kokedama is completely covered.

Dirty moss

If you like the idea of green sheet moss or grass colonizing your kokedama and want to speed up the natural process, then this technique is for you.

You will need
1 plant
Sphagnum moss
Bonsai moss spores
Grass seed (optional)

For this technique you are going to incorporate the spores of lush green sheet moss (and grass seed if you would like) into the sphagnum moss that you use to make the kokedama.

After you have soaked and drained the sphagnum moss, add a packet of bonsai moss spores and mix thoroughly. If you want grass, add a couple of tablespoons of lawn grass seed too.

Sphagnum is a great host substrate; grass germination should begin within days, and moss within weeks.

Initially the ball looks more "dirty" than if you use straight sphagnum, but it will green up much more quickly and you have

the bonus of avoiding the awkward teenage fungi phase altogether (see page 32).

Because you are speeding up the naturalization process it is best to use a synthetic twine or nylon to wrap the ball, even if you then cover it with natural twine. The natural twine may decompose more quickly than it would normally. The roots of the plant will not have had time to grow through the ball enough to hold it all together. Once the sheet moss starts to colonize the surface, it will cover the string too.

Right, above and below: The contents of a packet of bonsai moss spores are added to the saturated sphagnum moss; the spores and their soil are mixed thoroughly through the moss

Fancy moss

This method creates a wild, overgrown and lush look. Try to find really voluminous and visually interesting moss to use.

You will need
1 kokedama
Fancy moss
Staple gun
Creeping vine (optional)

Just as with the sheet moss technique, you are going to stick fancy moss to the outside of an already made-up kokedama of your choice. Keep in mind that the plant will need to have similar environmental requirements as the moss. The moss will require daily misting and regular soaking. It will also need fairly low and constant temperatures. Take some pieces of fancy moss and staple them to the kokedama. Try to use as few staples as possible to get the job done, so you don't end up with a Frankenstein's monster situation.

Use different types of moss to make a mosaic of texture and colour. Make it dense so the final effect is rich and luscious.

For an extra wild style, wrap the ball with a creeping vine such as New Zealand white rata or creeping fig (*Ficus pumila*). Look for vines with tiny leaves to give a sense of scale.

Right, above and below: A varied selection of lush decorative live moss is being stapled in place; a creeping vine (white rata) is being tied around the ball as a finishing touch to the wild look

CARING FOR YOUR KOKEDAMA

Kokedama, in theory, are simple to care for.
The trick is providing the right care for the
plant you have chosen and the specific
environment you have in your home.
Each plant and home will be different.

All plants require food, water and sunlight to survive. Different plants will require different amounts of each. Make sure you choose a plant which will thrive on the level of light and care you can provide. Most indoor plants prefer a humid atmosphere and indirect light.

Kokedama are not a magical water-producing form. They are basically just a very good – and good-looking – pot. Moss works slightly better than terracotta in that it is less prone to wicking moisture out of the soil. So although wrapping your plant in moss doesn't produce water per se, each plant should require less watering than it would if it was kept in a terracotta pot of the same size.

There are many additional benefits to using a wrapped ball instead of a pot. For example when plants are kept inside, they miss out on the cleansing experience of wind and rain. Dust and other contaminants build up on the leaves and will eventually form a barrier to light. To get rid of this dusty coating, fully submerge the whole plant and ball in a bath or laundry tub using tepid soft water and swoosh the leaves around. Alternatively, gently wash under the shower with tepid water. Because all the soil is contained within the ball you don't have to worry about it coming out of the pot and making a mess or disappearing.

One thing to be mindful of is which string you use to bind your balls. All natural fibres will break down over time. More water and more light will speed this process up. Be prepared to re-wrap, or alternatively use a synthetic twine or fishing nylon.

Opposite: Stenocactus wrapped with sphagnum and jute twine

Watering

Weight is a good way to tell when your hanging plant requires water; lift the ball in your hand – if it feels light, watering is needed. Getting to know these signs will help you establish a good routine.

Plants will often tell you if they are thirsty – some will droop, some will curl up the edges of their leaves, and succulents will start to get wrinkly and weird. Suspended kokedama require a bit more attention but don't let this put you off, as watering is super easy.

Watering

Fill a sink or bucket halfway with water. If using a bucket, place in the bath or the shower base to avoid drips and splashes.

Place your kokedama into the water. If the ball is very dry, it will float on the surface. Ideally the plant should absorb enough water to completely saturate the moss

Left: The leaves of *Calathea rufibarba* before and after watering *Opposite:* A group of kokedama being watered in a bathroom sink

ball, causing it to sink. Depending on the size and dryness of the ball, this can take anywhere from 10 to 30 minutes. Once the ball is fully saturated, remove from the water and allow water to drain away for another 30 minutes. This will reduce unwanted drips when you rehang it. Remember to water more frequently during summer when temperatures are higher and humidity is lower. In winter, water less frequently to avoid root rot. Misting your kokedama lightly between watering will ensure your plant and moss love you the most!

Feeding

Most plants require feeding at least once every season. The best way to do this is to buy a good quality organic liquid fertilizer and add it to the water as per the instructions on the packet. Try to avoid chemically produced or artificial fertilizers as they can be harmful to waterways.

More detailed information about specific plant feeding requirements is listed with each plant group.

Naturalization and restoration

If using a natural twine to wrap your kokedama, at some point the twine will begin to decay. This is to be expected from an organic material, and is part of the naturalization process. This leads in time to a ball that has its own moss ecosystem and is held in shape by its own roots. Different plants need different environments, so kokedama don't all naturalize at the same rate.

Ages and stages

The first stage of naturalization is normally colonization of the surface by fungi. These guys are the first step in the biodegrading process. They get in among the surfaces of natural materials and send tendrils through and start to break the materials apart. In the wild, this process is incredibly important as it allows all the other natural processes to begin. It prepares surfaces for other organisms, such as moss, to colonize. Once the fungi have finished, moss comes along and covers the surface in beautiful lush green.

Plan of attack

Depending on your situation and placement of your kokedama, this fungal process may not be ideal. Even though it is an important function in the wild, it can be confronting in the home environment. Yet fungi found on a kokedama will be almost without exception harmless to humans and pets.

There are several paths one can take when a kokedama reaches his awkward teenage phase of weird blemishes and unsightly surfaces. The first option is to let him do his thing and trust that eventually he will come out the other side and be a spectacular moss-covered beauty. Keep in mind though that if your ball is kept inside he won't be exposed to wild moss spores. You may have to give him a helping hand by purchasing bonsai moss spores and painting them onto the ball like a delicious mud-moss facial mask. You could also completely disguise the process by covering the whole ball with a sheet of moss or pieces of fancy moss (see pages 24–7).

You could also restore him to his pre-fungi glory. Remove the decaying string, add another layer of fresh sphagnum and retie the ball with new twine. The type of plant and how much moisture the twine is exposed to will determine the frequency of this process.

Left: A kokedama which has been kept outdoors and colonized by local sheet moss *Opposite:* Decomposed string on a succulent kokedama

TROPICALS

Environment
and care

Above, left and right: Monstera deliciosa gets his leaves washed in a tepid shower;
juvenile leaves of a *Monstera deliciosa* are gently wiped with a damp cloth

Tropical plants in this section have been chosen for their high-impact lush green foliage. There are many more plants in this category and most of them will be highly suitable to life as a kokedama.

IN A KOKEDAMA?

The thing to remember about tropical plants is that they love humidity. In the wild they would have lovely warm humid air interspersed with heavy deluges of rain. They would be growing in rich organic matter or in rich soil. You will notice that the following plants have soil recipes which replicate the forest floor environment they hail from.

Left: A collection of tropical kokedama being soaked in a bathtub

RECOMMENDED ROOM

A bright room out of direct sun will be ideal. Some of these plants will tolerate lower light conditions so won't need to be so close to windows. Any room where there is sunlight coming in through the window for more than 3 hours a day should suffice for most, unless specifically noted.

RECOMMENDED WATERING METHOD

Because most tropical plants are large, the ball of the kokedama will by necessity also be fairly large. This is great because the humidity in the ball will stay high for longer.

Soak your kokedama often in summer but allow drying out on the surface between soaking. Reduce soaking in winter and allow the ball to dry out by 2 thirds between watering.

Mist foliage often, even as often as daily, but do so in the morning rather than the evening.

Dust and other airborne contaminants will build up on the surface of large leaves. This makes it harder for light to penetrate the leaves and will need to be removed either with a dampened soft cloth or by gently washing leaves with tepid water under a shower.

Large fibre kokedama

Most of the soil recipes in this section include coconut mulch. This lovely product is totally brilliant inside the kokedama of tropical plants because it allows pockets of moist air to form. As coconut mulch is made of large chunks it can be tricky to work within the quantities required for some of the larger plants. Use a bowl to house all the elements of your creation as you go.

Remember the moss wants to be as thick as possible for tropical plants. Due to the high humidity, tropical plants are prime candidates for rapid deterioration of natural fibres used for wrapping. Either use a synthetic twine or reinforce with nylon fishing line underneath the natural twine layer. I used nylon in this project over the top of the string and hidden within the compressed moss. Nylon may be used for the first step also but you might find it a bit fiddly.

Left: An anthurium has been tied using the bowl method *Overleaf, left and right:* An anthurium wrapped with dried sphagnum and flax fibre parcel twine; an anthurium, a schefflera and a philodendron hang above a porch

1. Tie several pieces of string together into one bundle with a knot in the middle of the lengths. You want the ends to hang over easily. Place the knot in the centre of the bowl and fan out the ends evenly.

2. Put a layer of moss on top of the string. Press down firmly to compress it and keep the bowl form. Place plant in the centre and fill around with soil mix. Cover top of root ball with more moss and press into place.

3. Take 2 ends of string from opposite sides of the bowl and tie them in the centre as firmly as possible. Repeat with the remaining string pairs. Remove ball from bowl. Wrap ball with chosen string type.

4. Big glossy leaves will probably get in your way. Utilize the edge of the table to get the leaves out of your working area and also protect them from being crushed during the wrapping process.

Anthurium andraeanum 'Otazu'
Flamingo flower

Family name
Araceae

Type
Foliage

Light
Moderate

Watering
Moderate to high

Growth speed
Moderate to fast

Pets
Mildly toxic to cats and dogs

Common concern
Lack of humidity

SOIL RECIPE
2 parts potting mix
1 part compost
1 part coconut mulch

One of the best choices of plants for kokedama, with lush and glossy leaves and stunning inflorescences which continue throughout the year, this is an easy plant to enjoy. Anthurium flowers come in hues in the red spectrum, from candy pink to deep blood red to almost black, and the leaves range from verdant frog green to a lush deep forest green. The biggest problem for anthuriums is their high demand for humidity. They don't like soggy roots so frequent watering is a no-go. To get them to produce their beautiful flowers, mist the foliage once or twice a day.

Growing conditions
As a tropical under-grower, anthurium is accustomed to dappled light filtering through the canopy overhead. He enjoys access to plenty of indirect light, but will get sunburned if rays directly touch the leaves. Don't keep him too far away from the light source because he will stretch his leaves towards it and become scraggy and weird. He does not enjoy low temperatures or cold draughts. Remove spent flowers.

Water and food
During spring while he is actively growing, make sure he has enough water to perpetually provide moisture to his hungry roots. Do not allow the ball to dry out more than half. Watering as often as once a week could be necessary during the warmer summer months, but this will be different for different size kokedama and is also environment-specific. Because he grows such big lush leaves, he needs to be fed at least once a fortnight during his spring growth spurt. Continue to water frequently through summer, but reduce during winter to avoid root rot. Although suspending the plant does alleviate some risk in regards to soggy roots, over-frequent watering is still one of the main issues for anthuriums.

Aspidistra elatior
Cast iron plant

Family name
Asparagaceae

Type
Foliage

Light
Low to moderate

Watering
Low to moderate

Growth speed
Slow

Pets
Pet friendly

Common concern
Overwatering

SOIL RECIPE
2 parts potting mix
1 part coconut mulch

An easy favourite as a kokedama, the cast iron plant is aptly named. Thriving on neglect, he will withstand poor conditions and survive where many others would fail. He tolerates low light and a huge temperature range, making him ideal as a transient. He will happily move from the bathroom to the lounge (living room) and then to the hallway. Totally not fussy but with a strong preference for not being touched on the roots, he will happily grow larger and larger in a kokedama for several years. Eventually his roots will have consumed the available space and he will cease his expansion, but will still be fine. You can if you wish dismantle the kokedama and split the plant into several smaller ones and make various new kokedama to keep – or to give away!

Growing conditions
During Victorian times when indoor gas lighting produced fumes fatal to most other plants, cast iron plants dominated the indoor plant scene. Don't be cruel to yours though, as providing good conditions will only cause him to flourish. He doesn't enjoy poor treatment, only withstands it better than others. Although he will not die if kept in a dark corner, he will not produce new growth. If he has access to a sunless window, such as in a guest bathroom or laundry, he will produce lovely new leaves. Don't put him in direct sunlight though as he is prone to leaf scorching. As to temperature, this is the one thing which you needn't worry about. He will flourish just as well in cold rooms as warm ones.

Water and food
Aspidistra requires only moderate access to moisture and will suffer badly from being watered too frequently. During the growing season (spring/summer), soak the ball well then allow to almost completely dry out before watering again. Add a good liquid fertilizer to every second bath to help with new growth. The time it takes will differ depending on position (meaning how much light and heat he is exposed to).

Monstera deliciosa
Swiss cheese plant

Family name
Araceae

Type
Climber (vine)

Light
Bright, filtered

Watering
Low

Growth speed
Slow

Pets
Toxic to cats and dogs

Common concern
Overwatering

SOIL RECIPE
2 parts compost
1 part coir
3 parts coconut mulch

Overleaf, left and right: Large
Monstera deliciosa thriving in the
bright indirect light of an east-facing
window; juvenile *Monstera deliciosa*
hang serene in a loft dining room

A true wild Amazonian beauty, this is the biggest leaf you are likely to see inside a house. Being a giant climber (vine), he does require some specialist support later on in life once he starts his creeping journey. Due to his wide tolerance, he can also continue to grow at his original size for many years; just prune him by chopping off his growing tip with a very sharp knife. If this is done below a growth node a new plant can be raised from this cutting. But if you want him to grow to his full viney size you will need to provide him with "branches" to grab onto. Without support he will break his stem under his own weight. Clip or tie him to the chain and he will grab onto it himself. It does make watering tricky once he has grown up the chain some distance. Use the flexitub method described in the tree section (see page 118).

Growing conditions
Monstera prefers bright indirect light, the kind he would get inside the jungle. He will tolerate low light conditions though, but won't grow as well. He is particularly well suited to the back corner of a room which isn't going to get too dark. Being a jungle dweller he loves humidity and warm temperatures. That being said, low humidity and low temperatures will just cause him to grow slowly. Because of the large surface area of the leaves, and lack of tropical monsoons, he will need your help to keep his foliage dusted. Use a soft damp cloth to gently clean his leaves if they seem lacklustre.

Water and food
His preference is high humidity but he will tolerate drier air. During summer he will expect summer monsoons, or random, massive amounts of water. Simulate this with the shower or bath. Allow the ball to dry out between watering, especially in winter. His aerial roots are for absorbing water so he will appreciate a little misting on these. During spring and summer when he does his main growing, feed him some organic liquid fertilizer with his water. This won't need to be as frequent as faster growing plants, but will increase as the plant becomes larger over the years.

Syagrus romanzoffiana
Queen palm

Family name
Arecaceae

Type
Palm

Light
Full sun

Watering
Low

Growth speed
Fast

Pets
Pet friendly

Common concern
Not enough light

SOIL RECIPE
2 parts potting mix
1 part coconut mulch
1 part coir

Not a plant commonly used as a houseplant, in the wild he would grow to about 15 metres (49 feet) tall. If kept in a kokedama indoors, he will stay relatively small. Compared with other plants in your home though, he's probably pretty big. The cool thing about this guy is he makes these amazing shield leaves which burst apart later on to create fluffy brush-like forms. So for a while he will provide this fantastic architectural form with big strong lines, then one day his leaves mature and they start this process of becoming a grown-up palm. He grows his trunk very straight and his leaf stems are very straight, too. When he makes his fluffy leaf move, he normally has the straight lines to pull it off and still stay pretty structural-looking.

Growing conditions
Hailing from tropical climates, this palm likes it hot. He is a giant of the jungle which is why he grows such a straight trunk. He heads straight for the top to all the light. If you want to keep him at a manageable size indoors, he needs at least 8 hours of full sun every day. If he gets less, he will start shooting upwards, searching for the sun at the top of the canopy he thinks is shading him. He will grow less in cooler conditions (as in not tropical hot) but that alone will not prevent him from trying to burst out of your ceiling.

Water and food
Soak this kokedama frequently but allow it to dry out slightly between watering. Mist leaves to help keep humidity up and keep his leaves glossy. He won't mind the occasional wash down in tepid water in the shower. Dust will otherwise accumulate on his leaves and gradually block out light. Use a good quality organic liquid fertilizer at half strength once a season to keep him lush. Too much fertilizer will burn his roots.

BULBS, CORMS
AND TUBERS

Environment and care

Although their above-ground display can be vastly different, plants that grow from bulbs, corms or tubers are all similar in that they all possess a fleshy organ from which roots are produced and where food is stored. This whole group can be split in 2: temporary and permanent displays. Temporary displays are just that – they will grow and flower for a week, or a month, then die down and will often become completely dormant. Permanent displays are plants which can produce foliage and often flowers for almost the entire year. These guys will happily stay in a kokedama for years before they need to be split and remade into new balls.

Left: A cyclamen wrapped with live green moss and tied with nylon is soaked in a shallow dish *Opposite:* The cyclamen should not become saturated all the way to the top – remove from dish when water reaches up to three quarters

IN A KOKEDAMA?

Daffodils, tulips, hyacinths, and certain scillas and crocuses can all be treated as temporary. The kokedama is best used as a floral display for these guys rather than a permanent home. Permanent displays will require some special care and attention. Most bulbs are very prone to rot due to their fleshy nature. To combat this make sure at least 1 third and up to half of the storage organ is free of moss and therefore exposed to the air.

RECOMMENDED ROOM

A bright room out of direct sun is ideal. Some of these plants will tolerate lower light conditions. Any room where there is sunlight coming in through the window for more than 3 hours should suffice for most unless specifically noted.

RECOMMENDED WATERING METHOD

Place the ball in a shallow dish and allow water to be absorbed from the bottom up. The ball should not become fully saturated; remove from dish when outside of ball feels moist over halfway up.

Seasonal bulb kokedama

For this project, a seasonal flowering bulb is made into a kokedama. Flowering bulbs provide a splash of colour that otherwise isn't available indoors. In this instance the bulbs were purchased already in flower. They will continue to flower for weeks and, in some cases, not only provide a beautiful display but also an intoxicating fragrance. Because they are so short-lived, these guys go all out to make sure you notice them. However, it is definitely a case of the sprint rather than the marathon. They do eventually run out of puff. Bulbs spend half the year in dormancy waiting for next year's show.

When making a flowering bulb into a kokedama, the standard process can be followed with each soil recipe for the different plants. The only, but very important, additional feature is to ensure that the actual bulbs remain exposed. The bulbs are very susceptible to rot and it will take hold very quickly once present.

Right: A daffodil has been bound using live green moss and fishing nylon

56

As you are forming the moss around the soil mixture and root ball, press gently but firmly with your thumbs around the bulbs. Keep doing this at each step so the ball ends up well below the top of the bulbs. Once all the wrapping is finished, do a final push down around the bulbs to really get them in the clear.

Keep this in mind when selecting a plant for your project. Look for big, well-formed, clean bulbs. Check that they have no signs of damage or disease.

The final part of this project is what to do with him after he has finished flowering. If throwing him in the compost doesn't appeal to you, then you have 2 options.

Either plant the whole lot outside in the garden, under a tree, to do its thing again next year.

Or, if you want to have a second year of indoor flowers, you will have to keep looking after him until all his leaves die down. Once all foliage has died, allow the ball to dry out completely. Store

Right: Pushing moss down around the bulbs to ensure they are fully exposed

somewhere cold, dry and dark. He will rest until spring.

Once the midwinter solstice has passed, bring him out and gently reintroduce him to the environment. Start by slightly dampening the ball and only increase water once he shows

signs of life. Give him a good feed of organic fertilizer in liquid form each week until he flowers. How well he flowers the second time will depend on how he was induced to flower the previous year. If he was forced, he may not flower again until the following year.

Cyclamen persicum
Persian cyclamen

Family name
Primulaceae

Type
Tuberous winter-flowering
perennial

Light
Moderate

Watering
Moderate

Growth speed
Moderate

Pets
Toxic to cats and dogs

Common concerns
Overheating, fungal growth on
spent flowers, tuber rot

SOIL RECIPE
1 part compost
1 part coir

Florists' cyclamen grow from a
tuber, with leaves and roots all
originating from the same bulb-
like structure. Their tubers should
only be half buried; complete
submersion will cause them to rot.
They are frost tender so can only
be kept indoors. However, being a
winter flowerer means that overly
warm temperatures can trigger
summer dormancy and will greatly
shorten the lifespan of flowers.

Growing conditions
These are one of the better
performers when looking for
indoor flower producers. You will
need to find the perfect spot to
achieve a constant gentle but
bright indirect light without any
noticeable upward temperature
changes. Cyclamen are prone
to fainting if they become even
slightly drier than their preferred
state. Conversely, overwatering
can cause instant death. If you
stick with him and find his required
rhythm of care, your plant will
produce seemingly endless
profusions of starburst flowers

above lush heart-shaped foliage
for months. Trim off spent flowers
promptly, to avoid the spread of
troublesome mould.

Water and food
Cyclamen are tricky to get right,
but worth it if you can manage
it. They don't like overwatering,
so soaking the ball is not
recommended. Instead, place
the ball in a shallow dish of water
and allow the water to be taken
up. Depending on location and
environmental humidity, this may
have to be done as frequently as
every second or third day. Misting
leaves in the morning can help,
but don't mist heavily, causing
run-off onto the tuber, and
don't allow water to sit on leaves
overnight. If leaves are still wet in
the evening, reduce the amount
given. Use liquid fertilizer added
to water every 1 to 2 weeks as per
instructions on the packet.

Narcissus 'Grand Soleil d'Or'
Tazetta daffodil

Family name
Amaryllidaceae

Type
Seasonal bulb

Light
Moderate

Watering
High

Growth speed
Very fast

Pets
Highly toxic to pets

Common concerns
Overheating, underwatering

SOIL RECIPE
2 parts perlite
1 part compost

Short and very sweet, if you want a high impact visual display for an event or for a brief period, then narcissi are perfect. Some come with such strong smells as to be cloying and suffocating when confined in a room with them. The one featured here has a subtle sweet and spicy scent. Once inside, narcissi cannot be forced to flower more than once in that year. After the flowers are finished, either discard the whole lot or plant it outside (choosing a sheltered spot for this particular daffodil). If you want to keep it in the ball, be warned that it may take up to 2 years to flower again. Don't cut the leaves off; they are important for feeding the bulb for next year's flowers. Keep watered and fed until all leaves have died away. Put the whole ball somewhere cold, dry and dark until spring. To regrow leaves from the ball in spring, soak in lightly fertilized water. Keep ball slightly moist until green tips appear, then increase watering to normal.

Growing conditions
Normally found under the eaves of big trees, on the edges of forests and among lush borders, narcissi prefer dappled shade while still having access to plenty of indirect light. Flowers tend to stretch towards the light source; this can add or detract from the aesthetic of your kokedama depending on how it is managed. It is possible to create interesting shapes if handled carefully, and equally possible to create lush bunches. When planting, make sure bulbs remain exposed as they are prone to rotting.

Water and food
Water from below by placing in a shallow dish and allowing the water to be taken up. Mist in the morning, but don't overdo it, just enough to mimic gentle dew. If the bulbs are not dried out during the day they will rot. Their roots need water but not the bulb. Never the bulb.

Overleaf, left and right: A cyclamen and a daffodil kokedama wrapped with live green moss and tied with nylon; cyclamen wrapped with flax fibre parcel twine and dried sphagnum

Oxalis triangularis
Purple shamrock

Family name
Oxalidaceae

Type
Clumping tuber

Light
Bright

Watering
Moderate

Growth speed
Fast

Pets
Mildly toxic

Common concerns
Overwatering, underwatering

SOIL RECIPE
1 part coir
1 part compost

Oxalis is a bit of a dark horse. He has this pretty cool magic trick where if you treat him bad, he will pretend to die. All his leaves will wilt down and he will hide in his bulb. Once he has finished sulking, normally because you have noticed his death faint and restored your love to him, he will pop back up good as new. Particularly useful for those little accidents where we forget to water our plants for several months at a time. If you discover a dry and desiccated ball with some shrivelled shamrock leaves, give him some water and a warm sunny spot and watch him resurrect himself like a phoenix.

Growing conditions
Oxalis is not particularly fussy about light, but won't tolerate full shade or full sun. Most positions in between will be fine. Temperature is more important. If he gets too cold he will faint. If he gets too much direct sun he will get sunburnt. One important thing about oxalis is that he doesn't like a tight ball. He only has tiny little fine roots which are basically feeble. If the ball is too dense and tight he won't be able to grow his roots and he will die.

Water and food
Ideally soak the kokedama and then allow the outside to dry to the touch before soaking again. Irregular and random watering actually doesn't really bother him. In fact he can probably go months without being adversely affected, especially during the cooler months. If he is in a very warm or very sunny spot you will need to make an effort to water regularly, because if he does get too dry, he will do his death faint trick.

Zantedeschia 'Blaze'
Calla lily

Family name
Araceae

Type
Clumping tuber

Light
Moderate to bright

Watering
High

Growth speed
Moderate

Pets
Highly toxic to cats and dogs

Common concern
Temperature fluctuation

SOIL RECIPE
3 parts coir
1 part compost
1 portion water crystals

Commonly referred to as a calla lily, he isn't a true lily; he is a distant relative, in fact a tuberous perennial. He has no central stem; instead he grows his lovely long-stemmed leaves in clumps directly from his tubers just below the surface. Keep this in mind when making up the kokedama and don't bury him too deep into the ball. Also allow room for new shoots by not wrapping the string too closely around the leaf stems. Once he has finished flowering, his leaves will die down and he will become dormant.

Growing conditions
He would normally grow in marshy or swampy ground in the wild so he likes his roots to be constantly wet. Because of the increased exposure to air when hanging, it is important to counteract any drying effect this would have by making a very moisture-rich soil, using plenty of moss and even a layer of coconut fibre if possible. Use a synthetic twine to avoid disintegration. The constant moisture will rot natural fibres very rapidly.

Water and food
Keep him wet and soggy. Soak as soon as the outside shows signs of drying. Soak overnight once a month during flowering period. Fertilize regularly with a good quality organic fertilizer. When he has a decent bunch of flowers, water once a week; before that stick to once a fortnight or less to avoid long flimsy stems.

If you want to keep him and have flowers a second time, the tubers have to be cared for over his dormant period. As his leaves begin to yellow and wilt, reduce watering frequency and eventually allow the ball to completely dry out. Leave the ball outside until autumn (fall), when the new growth period begins, ensuring the plant is not frosted. Bring indoors and slowly increase available water until he has plenty of leaves and flowers, then resume regular saturation.

SUCCULENTS
AND CACTI

Environment and care

Opposite: A group of succulents absorbing water in a sink *Above:* Spiderwebs are being removed from cactus pricks

All cacti are succulent, but not all succulents are cacti. Lots of plant families have 1 or 2 members who are succulent even if the rest of them are shrub-like or herbaceous. There are 2 basic types of succulent: the guys who store water in their leaves and those who store water in their stems. Cacti are the biggest family of succulents and they store water in their stems. The rest mostly have thick fleshy leaves where they store water – they are basically the camels of the plant world.

IN A KOKEDAMA?
Perfect for hanging kokedama because he isn't sitting in a dish of stagnant and stale water waiting for his roots to rot. Succulents tend to suffer from very rapid onset root rot if exposed to too much water. They need the water to drain away from their roots, so make sure to include perlite or similar to help the water pass through. Unlike other plants which need humidity, these guys prefer a bit of dry, with the exception of jungle cacti, who although don't like anywhere near as much water as other jungle plants, won't complain about the occasional misting.

RECOMMENDED ROOM
The brightest, hottest room is the place for these guys. The room which is most like a desert. If you notice your plant getting a long, central stem with widely spaced leaves, especially in varieties which should be rosette shaped, he isn't getting enough light. He thinks he is being shaded by surrounding plants and is trying to grow up to the top of their canopy to get to the light. If he looks "leggy" move him somewhere sunnier.

RECOMMENDED WATERING METHOD
Soak him once a month. When you put him into water, he should float and bob around on the surface like a cork. If he sinks straight away, he is probably not ready to be watered. The exception to this rule is the jungle cacti group. They prefer to keep a bit of humidity, but because of their aerial roots won't mind it a little dry. Leave your cactus in the water until he is fully saturated then let him drip dry. Premature rehanging will result in drips all over the place. Feed infrequently so as not to encourage excessive growth.

Cactus kokedama

By far the best plants when learning the art of kokedama. They are so forgiving and they basically thrive on neglect. They don't mind having their roots messed around with and they don't ever complain about being over-handled. This is great because it means if you don't like what you have made, you can take it apart and start again without upsetting anybody. Begin with non-prickly first and once you have the technique, move on to prickly cacti. The other great thing about these guys is that they look so good in little groups, so you can happily make to your heart's content without worrying about where to put them all. One window is plenty big enough.

Left: A pachycereus tied with dried moss and jute twine

1. Fold the prickly part of the plant in a piece of paper to protect your fingers. Gently work him out of his pot using the ends of the paper. Pinch the 2 ends together so the plant is held firmly within the paper.

2. Continue as you would normally but with extra care given to not touching him on the prickles.

3. When wrapping, it really is better to go tight for cacti and succulents. Because they will be left to totally dry out, the moss will shrink more than on other plants.

4. If the string is not tied firmly it can give a sort of saggy look to it or just fall off. Avoid the embarrassment of saggy string by applying plenty and tightly.

Echeveria elegans
Mexican gem

Family name
Crassulaceae

Type
Succulent

Light
Bright

Watering
Low

Growth speed
Moderate

Pets
Mildly toxic

Common concerns
Overwatering, root rot
and mealy bugs

SOIL RECIPE
1 part potting mix
1 part perlite

Overleaf, left and right: Assorted
echeveria hang above a bed; rhipsalis
and lepismium on hooks in a scullery

Echeveria is easily the most common succulent sold as house plants. Purely for the reasons of being an absolute breeze to care for and offering so many varied forms of colour and texture. Often the leaves will have a wax or pale bloom coating their surface. Keep in mind this can be easily damaged if handled. Most echeveria will flower indoors, producing long stems with delicate and often incredibly intricate bell-shaped profusions at the end.

Growing conditions
Echeveria elegans is a long-time favourite for kokedama. He is so tolerant. He really doesn't mind having his roots disturbed at all, so he is great for learning how to make kokedama with.

Once actually in a kokedama he only needs a soak once a month. Occasional misting in between times if you can manage it is nice but he still probably won't complain if you forget. He loves a good sunny spot and will reward you with a blush of pink across his leaf tips, but indirect light is also fine. He will just stay his lovely turquoise green.

When making this guy up, be sure to use a very firm hand when wrapping and use plenty of string. As he dries out between watering the moss itself dries and shrinks. If you have used a loose wrapping style the string may come off the ball or sag unattractively.

Water and food
Water by soaking until saturated once a month in summer and less in winter. Exact timing will depend on the size of the ball and climate of the house. If leaves start to appear wrinkled he needs a drink. Definitely err on the side of too dry, however. Overwatering will cause root and stem rot very quickly. You will get the feel for when he has dried out enough. The ball will be very pale and almost weightless.

Feed during spring, but only use a half-strength organic liquid fertilizer.

Lepismium houlletianum Snowdrop cactus

Family name
Cactaceae

Type
Jungle cactus

Light
Moderate

Watering
Moderate

Growth speed
Fast

Pets
Pet friendly

Common concern
Sun scorching

SOIL RECIPE
1 part potting mix
1 part compost
1 part perlite

As a member of the genus *Lepismium*, the snowdrop cactus is found in jungles, not in deserts. He is ideal for kokedama, as he likes to be up high and likes to have lots of air around him. He doesn't require huge amounts of light in order to thrive and is very, very easy to care for. He grows flowers along the edges of his flat "leaves" (stems, strictly speaking), producing them from the spiky bits towards the tip. He is perfect for hanging further back in a room where sunbeams won't scorch him. He won't tolerate total darkness, but he will tolerate much shadier situations than many other flowering plants.

Growing conditions
Preferring to grow in the shade or dappled filtered light, these guys should never be exposed to direct sunlight, or their leaves will go weird and wrinkly and sometimes acquire a red tinge. Because of their jungle origins, they don't like dry air, so mist often to keep leaf moisture up. They don't particularly like extreme temperatures; too hot or too cold will cause them to sulk. When in a sulk they are very susceptible to invasion by pests or disease.

Water and food
These jungle cacti should not be allowed to dry out completely. During spring and summer, when they are busy growing, they will need to have access to high levels of moisture. Soak your cactus ball frequently at this time of year, keeping it moist but not soggy. Mist his leaves frequently with soft water if possible. Because of the wide flat surface of his leaves he will need a bath occasionally or a rinse in the shower to remove surface build-up of dust.

Feed with a good quality liquid fertilizer in with his water during the growing season. Reduce watering and feeding in winter, allowing ball to dry somewhat between soaking.

Rhipsalis cereuscula
Coral cactus

Family name
Cactaceae

Type
Jungle cactus

Light
Moderate

Watering
Low to moderate

Growth speed
Moderate

Pets
Pet friendly

Common concern
Sun scorching

SOIL RECIPE
1 part potting mix
1 part compost
1 part perlite

Rhipsalis are cacti, but they are found in jungles rather than the desert. They make an ideal candidate for kokedama because they love being up in the breeze. They are super easy to care for and somewhat forgiving of minor neglect. They are made of little segments joined together, and these will break off easily if knocked. So be gentle with your rhipsalis. He doesn't need to be right up at a window; he will do fine further back in the room where there is less light.

Growing conditions
Because his leaf-like stems are succulent (water storing) he is somewhat drought tolerant, but don't overdo it. He is a thirsty cactus. He would normally grow in the jungle, shaded by all the plants above him. He would get dappled sunlight at most, or occasionally if he was growing at the edge of the jungle a bit more. Although he isn't prone to sunburn, exposure to direct sunlight will cause a red tinge on his tips, or in extreme cases, the little segments can get wrinkly. What he really likes is a

summer vacation to a shady spot outside. Hanging from a big tree is perfect. This will encourage lush growth and may even prompt flowering.

Water and food
This guy stores water in his leaf segments. So although he can survive drought conditions normally, during his growth period he needs extra water to fill up all his new leaf segments. Like water balloons. Don't expose new growth to harsh conditions as the skin is very fragile, like a newborn.

He loves a regular misting on his leaves. Allow the ball to dry out somewhat between watering in winter.

Feed him with a good quality organic liquid fertilizer during his growing season. Use at half strength added to soaking water every second soak.

EPIPHYTES

Environment
and care

Epiphytes are plants which, in the wild, grow rooted onto the body of another plant or on rocks. Epiphytes use aerial roots to cling onto their support and gain nourishment from the atmosphere or from the crevices where they reside. Although they cling onto other plants, epiphytes are not parasitic – they do not damage their host plant.

They love warm moist air with the occasional good soaking. Most don't enjoy water sitting on their flowers though, so keep this in mind when soaking.

IN A KOKEDAMA?

The non-parasitic relationship is key to understanding why these plants do so well in a kokedama. By enclosing his aerial roots in a lovely humid atmosphere where they are protected from dramatic temperature changes, the epiphyte thinks he has found

Left: Air plants are soaked in a bowl of water

the most idyllic spot ever to grow. Because he won't have to put any energy into finding a good spot to grow, he can focus all his attention on being an absolutely stunning specimen. As long as his ball doesn't get too much or too little water, your epiphyte will be the happiest epiphyte in town!

RECOMMENDED ROOM

A bright room out of direct sun will be ideal. A lounge (living room) or conservatory are perfect options as they normally have windows in multiple walls, increasing the light in the room significantly.

Because epiphytes would normally grow on the trunk or in the fork of a tree, or nestled into a rock crevice, try to provide similar lighting conditions. In the wild epiphytes wouldn't usually be exposed to very much direct sun; they would probably get all-day diffused or dappled light.

RECOMMENDED WATERING METHOD

Unlike regular terrestrial plants, epiphytes generally collect water and nutrition via their leaves. Their watering and feeding regime will consist of two parts: foliar and root methods. During the growing season and hot months, foliar watering (misting) could be up to every second day to achieve optimum results. That being said, they do need to feel secure about the housing of their roots. If the kokedama dries out too frequently, he might decide he needs to explore his surroundings to find somewhere better to live. If he does do this, all his energy will go into making roots and not foliage or flowers.

Moisten your kokedama ball by standing it in water 1 third of the height of the ball and allow the water to soak up into it. Don't leave him over-long like this; an hour is usually sufficient. Allow the water to drain back out before rehanging. This only needs to be done monthly, if not less often.

Orchid kokedama

Keep in mind that most epiphytes use their roots primarily to hold onto stuff. Some, such as orchids, have a water-absorbing covering on their roots, while others such as elkhorns (staghorn ferns) develop a dense mat of roots that traps water to be released up to the leaves as humidity. Air plants are the extreme, as they don't require any soil at all.

The trick with epiphytes is to provide a cozy home for them with lots of humidity and no sitting water, plenty of airflow, and warm temperatures.

Due to the high proportion of large chunks in the mix for orchids, this technique requires some dexterity. If you find it too fiddly, try using the bowl method described for tropical plants (see page 39). Adding a layer of coconut fibre on the outside helps to reduce evaporation of moisture from within the ball.

Right: Orchid wrapped using coconut fibre over the moss

1. For all epiphytes use a coarse organic fibre such as coconut mulch to provide spaces for air and to assist the water to drain away.

2. Make a pancake of moss and place soil mixture in the centre. Place plant on top and gently fold moss up around to enclose. Compress moss and secure with string.

3. Once plant is secure in his moss, spread coconut fibre to wrap him in. The coconut fibre doesn't prevent liquid water from leaving the ball but it helps the air inside stay lovely and humid for the roots.

4. Secure the fibre and wrap in preferred style. Try to be firm but not crushing. If the orchid has crazy roots going everywhere, leave them on the outside of the ball.

Aechmea fasciata
Urn plant

Family name
Bromeliaceae

Type
Epiphyte

Light
Bright

Watering
Low

Growth speed
Moderate

Pets
Pet friendly

Common concerns
Urn drying out, urn water
stagnating

SOIL RECIPE
1 part coconut mulch
1 part coir
1 part perlite

Most aechmea grow as epiphytes in the wild, in humid tropical areas. The leaves are designed to catch and hold water as it falls from above. There is a cup in the centre which should always have water in it. Aechmea have absolutely spectacular flowers once the plant matures. Each rosette of leaves will send out a flower, which can bloom for weeks and sometimes months. After the flower has finished the whole rosette will die back. It's important to cut this old rosette off at the base with a sharp knife to allow room for the new growth.

Growing conditions
Aechmea need full sunlight to produce flowers; if they are kept too far from a window they will only have the foliage. Aechmea prefer warm temperatures and high humidity. The incorporation of coarse bark into the soil mix helps to provide adequate airflow through the ball.

Water and food
They have roots but they use them primarily to hang onto trees or rocks. Keep that central cup in mind when you water your aechmea: he likes to be watered from above, so put the whole kokedama in a sink or bucket and tip water continuously down into his cup. Let it overflow for a bit to clean it out. In the wild this would be done during monsoons or heavy rain events.

Aechmea do require regular feeding, but only half-strength. When administering food, use an organic liquid fertilizer and tip slowly over leaves and into central cup so that it falls into the bucket, where it can also be soaked up by the kokedama ball.

x *Oncostele* Wildcat 'Magic Leopard' Hybrid orchid

Family name
Orchidaceae

Type
Flowering epiphyte

Light
Moderate

Watering
Low to moderate

Growth speed
Slow

Pets
Pet friendly

Common concerns
Overwatering, underwatering, underfeeding, mildew

SOIL RECIPE
3 parts coconut mulch
1 part potting mix

Overleaf, left and right:
Odontocidiums hang above a bed; odontoglossums hang under a staircase in the reflected glow of afternoon sun

Many orchids are hybrids, combining the beauty of one type with the lush fragrance of another. It is well worth a conversation with an expert or local grower to find your perfect orchid match. Supermarket (grocery store) orchids are fine for "get well" gifts, but to truly experience the pleasure orchids have to offer, a foray into the deep is required.

Growing conditions
To get optimal growth from your orchid keep him in bright indirect light. Sunbeams straight onto him will scorch his delicate structures. Originating in tropical rainforests, growing in the forks of forest giants, these guys like occasional heavy watering and constant high humidity. They absorb water through their strange, grey, creeping, aerial roots. Even though they don't grow in soil, in the wild the roots would be growing into tree debris, fallen leaves and bark. Replicate this environment inside your kokedama. He loves to have a tight space to occupy that doesn't get too soggy and has plenty of organic matter to explore. Air circulation around the foliage and flower spikes is also highly important. During the warmer months, simply open the windows to increase ventilation. When it's colder, use a fan on low to keep air moving.

Water and food
Water when the ball has dried out. Keep in mind that the ball has a lot of empty space so doesn't hold as much water as soil-based balls. Mist foliage in the morning but do not allow to stay wet overnight. Use a specialized orchid food during flowering according to the instructions on the packet. Remember not to neglect your orchid when he is dormant, though. He is busy on the inside getting ready for the next flowers.

Platycerium bifurcatum
Staghorn fern

Family name
Polypodiaceae

Type
Epiphyte

Light
Bright

Watering
Moderate

Growth speed
Moderate

Pets
Pet friendly

Common concern
Drying out

SOIL RECIPE
1 part coir
1 part chopped sphagnum moss

This guy is such a great choice for hanging kokedama. He grows high up on trees, so loves being up in the air and will enjoy the increased airflow of being suspended. He is happy to take moisture from the air and use his roots for hanging on instead. He has a lovely silvery velvet covering on his leaves, which fan out like the antlers of a moose. He also has a shield leaf which is slightly different from his upward leaves. This shield leaf grows from the base of the plant and is partly for holding on and partly for feeding. Try to take care of it as it is very easily damaged by dropping the ball. It is made of a spongy material which snaps and breaks off fairly easily. If broken, a new one will grow; but lack of a shield leaf can impact the growth of the upward fronds.

Growing conditions
Direct morning sun or all-day indirect sun are best. Strong direct sun will cause weird discoloration on the leaves. These guys can tolerate fairly high temperatures as long as they don't dry out too much. In winter, they shouldn't be exposed to temperatures below 13°C (55°F), to avoid leaf drop.

Water and food
This fern loves to be misted frequently, sometimes as often as daily if the room is warm and dry. During spring and summer his ball needs to be soaked until saturated and then allowed to dry out almost completely. In the wild, he would use his shield leaf not just for hanging on with, but also for trapping debris and water to break down for food. You can replicate the accumulation of debris by adding some good quality liquid organic fertilizer to his water every second watering.

Overleaf: A large staghorn is displayed in two different locations

Tillandsia aeranthos
Air plant

Family name
Bromeliaceae

Type
Epiphyte

Light
Bright

Watering
Moderate

Growth speed
Slow

Pets
Pet friendly

Common concern
Leaves drying out

SOIL RECIPE
Just moss

Tillandsias are easy to care for. Hailing from Central and South American forests and jungles, they are survivors. They do have roots, but not for water, only to cling onto trees and the faces of cliffs. They don't require soil; just make a ball of moss directly onto the stem. This is more aesthetic than functional as they get all their water via the leaves. The foliage needs regular drenching and high humidity.

Growing conditions
Try to imagine these guys growing up high under the canopy of jungle trees. They wake up to the gentle early morning sunbeams peeking in under the treetops. They spend most of the day basking in dappled sunlight. The humidity rising up from all the trees and plants around and below them provides them with plenty of moisture, so they don't have to worry about finding wet soil. They will get burned very quickly if exposed to direct sunlight. Just look at that pale complexion!

Water and food
Tillandsias have water cells in their leaves which need to be completely filled when watering. Mist yours daily, and soak whole plant and ball for 10 minutes each week. Completely submerge in deep water. Soak him, dunk him or run him under a tap (faucet) to totally saturate his leaves. After weekly soaking leave him upside down to allow water to drain out of the centre. Sitting water left inside can lead to rot. Tillandsias kept in hot sunny rooms may need misting as frequently as every day. Use a very weak solution of organic fertilizer once a month to speed up growth and encourage flowers. Too much fertilizer (nutrients) can quickly kill tillandsias, so less is more.

FERNS

Environment and care

Ferns are the kings of foliage. They don't even bother with flowers or seeds. They focus 100% on being the lushest and most spectacular display of green in town. As with succulents, there are lots of plant families that can be described as "ferns" even though they are not genetically related. They are so similar in their growth habits and environmental requirements, that they may as well be. The exception is the asparagus fern, which isn't actually a fern per se because he does produce tiny flowers and then berries with seeds. However he is a firm favourite so mustn't be left out in the cold simply because he reproduces incorrectly.

IN A KOKEDAMA?
Ferns love humidity. You will see that most of the soil recipes include coir. This is a very dense water-retaining material made from ground up coconut husks.

It holds its water and releases it slowly as humidity without being a soggy mess. Most ferns are also going to want a really thick layer of moss. Due to their high humidity requirement they are a great candidate for live moss coverings. Moss needs heaps of humidity, ferns need heaps of humidity – boom, you have the perfect marriage!

RECOMMENDED ROOM
Ferns are ground dwellers, lounging on the forest floor and basking in the soft diffused light filtering down through the vast canopy above. Most ferns won't tolerate total shade and will be okay in quite bright light as long as it isn't hot direct sun. They can be hung slightly further back into rooms and will tolerate bathroom light because of the increased humidity on offer.

RECOMMENDED WATERING METHOD
Mist, mist, mist. Then mist some more. Especially if you have used live green moss to cover the ball, he needs a light mist every morning to keep both fern and moss happy. If possible, use a distilled water to prevent salts from damaging delicate leaves. Soak when ball begins to dry. Give leaves a bath occasionally to remove surface build-up. Swish him around under water but be gentle – some ferns, like the maidenhair, have stems which are easily snapped.

Opposite: Daily misting keeps ferns very happy

Fern kokedama

Typically found on forest floors, their soil mixture should include plenty of organic matter and coarse fibre. Ferns love growing under or on the rotting carcass of fallen trees, so try to imagine and replicate this kind of environment for them. A portion of coconut mulch is a good tree corpse substitute. It takes longer to break down than ordinary wood chips but still provides the same humid atmosphere for fern roots. They just love exploring stuff with their little creeping roots, so having a good texture inside the ball helps them to feel like they have found a great home. The other guy who loves a good tree carcass is moss. Moss and ferns are actually best buds. If you can harvest some live moss from a nearby forest or damp backyard (with landowner's permission), use it to wrap up Mr Fern and they will live happily ever after.

Right: A davallia has been wrapped using live green moss and fishing nylon

1. Ferns like it moist. Mix all the ingredients for the soil recipe together then make a mud pie.

2. Add enough water so that the mixture can be formed easily into a ball and hold its shape.

3. Make a ball of mud and chunks around the root ball of the fern. Keep in mind that the size of the ball will somewhat define the ultimate size of the fern. Bigger ball equals bigger fern.

4. Place the mud ball on moss. If using wild moss put it green side down on the table and put the ball on what would have been the underside of the moss. Use nylon to wrap, or another synthetic fibre.

Adiantum raddianum
Maidenhair fern

Family name
Pteridaceae

Type
Rhizomatous fern
(surface-creeping)

Light
Bright

Watering
Moderate

Growth speed
Moderate

Pets
Pet friendly

Common concerns
Underwatering followed
by overwatering

SOIL RECIPE
3 parts coir
1 part compost
1 part perlite

Once the correct routine is established and the perfect position found for him, he will reward you with a profusion of delicate soft foliage. Very hard to kill, if kept watered, this crusader will bounce back from most catastrophes. If he does suffer an "accidental drought" and his leaves die, do not be tempted to soak him. Cut off all his wilting foliage at the ball even if it means only 1 or 2 stalks are left. Then he can put all his energy into making new shoots. If you soak him at this point there won't be enough foliage to draw the moisture up away from the roots and they will rot. Lightly mist the top of the ball daily until you see new growth, then give a brief soak. Once he has a decent amount of foliage you can resume regular care.

Growing conditions
This guy is another dappled light lounger. He likes lots of light, without actual sunbeams touching his foliage and ruining his complexion. He will tolerate lower light conditions but watering must be reduced to account for a slower metabolism and avoid rot. His roots need to have access to humid moisture but not sitting water. He really dislikes cold draughts and will sulk if exposed to them. He sends out creeping shoots just below the surface and pops up new shoots all over the ball. If one is patient eventually this can be one of the most spectacular examples of kokedama.

Water and food
Do not allow to dry out. Give small amounts of water often to keep his moisture even. He loves a good misting on his leaves or a bath to wash his foliage. He will need regular feeding to support new growth. Feed fortnightly with a half-strength organic liquid fertilizer during summer but reduce in winter. Add 1 or 2 tablespoons of Epsom salts to 4.5 litres (1.2 US gallons) of water and use every 6 months to improve leaf colour.

Asparagus densiflorus 'Myersii' Foxtail fern

Family name
Asparagaceae

Type
Rhizomatous perennial

Light
Bright

Watering
High

Growth speed
Moderate to fast

Pets
Highly toxic

Common concern
Leaf drop

SOIL RECIPE
2 parts compost
1 part potting mix
1 part coir
1 part coconut mulch

He is not technically a fern, and he doesn't produce tasty asparagus spears like his edible cousin. He is actually a relative of the lily.

He looks and acts so much like a fern though, that it is appropriate to lump him in with ferns.

Unlike other plants, he won't necessarily see confined spaces as a reason to stay small. Keeping him suspended in kokedama form will limit this vigorous activity somewhat, however if you provide him with growth levels of water and food, he will continue to grow bigger. If he outgrows his ball, it won't be possible to keep up with his water requirements. Find the level that keeps him lush but lets him know there isn't enough water for adventure. Given his propensity to obesity, make the ball initially with a good proportion to the existing foliage and aim to keep him this size.

Growing conditions
This guy is great for bathrooms where the light is indirect and the humidity is high. He will tolerate a range of light, within reason. Too dark and he will get leggy stems and sparse foliage. Too much direct sun and he will get burned leaves. But everything in between is fine. He has little pine-needle leaves (actually cladodes) which he does sometimes shed in a very unthoughtful way, all over the place, if something is wrong.

Water and food
Because he has such long bushy and lush fronds, he uses a lot of water. Give him plenty but be careful not to over-fatten him. Because of his tendency towards obesity, be careful with the feeding. Give him liquid fertilizer at half the strength recommended on the packet. As above, if he outgrows his ball he will quickly dry out and die.

Overleaf, left and right: Asparagus 'Myersii' and davallia ferns hanging in a downstairs hang out; davallia and Boston ferns complete the tranquil desk of artist Amanda Fitzsimmons

Asplenium nidus
Bird's nest fern

Family name
Aspleniaceae

Type
Rosette-forming fern

Light
Moderate

Watering
Moderate

Growth speed
Moderate

Pets
Pet friendly

Common concern
Central core rot if overwatered

SOIL RECIPE
3 parts compost
1 part coconut mulch
1 part coir

Beautiful apple green leaves, glossy and rich, cluster together to form an upwards-spreading rosette, making a stunning shape when in a kokedama. He is a very large specimen. Because his leaves are so big, he will accumulate dust on them. It is possible to wipe each leaf with a dampened soft cloth but there is also the bath option. Fill up a bath with enough water to submerge the entire leaf mass and do so. Swish the leaves around under water to give them a good clean. Using the shower is also a great way to give him a hair wash. Just make sure the water is tepid in either scenario.

Growing conditions
Found nestled under or on tropical rainforest trees, the bird's nest fern loves a mild environment. Make sure he has plenty of indirect light to keep his leaves lush. Hang him near a sunless window, like a bathroom or hallway (entryway); just make sure there aren't any cold draughts tickling under his leaves. He doesn't mind lower temperatures, but won't grow as actively as he would in a warm room. Humidity is key – don't keep him in the same room as a dehumidifier or air conditioning unit as this will dry him out very quickly.

Water and food
Water often during the growth period so as not to let the ball dry out too much; he really wants to have constant access to lots of moisture. He loves a good frequent misting regime! Keep the mister near his spot so each time you pass you can give his leaves a good spritz.

Avoid letting water build up within his central core. If his leaves remain in contact with water for periods longer than 24 hours, they will begin to decompose.

Liquid fertilizer in with his water once a month during the growing period should be enough, but reduce to only one feed during the autumn (fall)/winter period. Reduce watering during winter months. These ferns will tolerate some drought during their dormancy but not indefinitely.

Davallia trichomanoides
Hare's foot fern

Family name
Davalliaceae

Type
Rhizomatous fern
(surface-creeping)

Light
Moderate

Watering
Moderate

Growth speed
Moderate to fast

Pets
Pet friendly

Common concern
None

SOIL RECIPE
3 parts compost
1 part coconut mulch
1 part coir

This guy is such a character! He has these crazy, fluffy tarantula-like rhizomes which creep along the surface. Even though he is known as hare, squirrel or rabbit's foot, the creeping tendrils really look like giant spider legs. When he's hanging in a kokedama, these creepy tendrils will trail down towards the ground. Either leave them like this or wrap them around the ball so they can put roots in. Any left outside the ball will grow new fronds even without roots, so your fern can end up creating quite a spectacle of creepy tendrils and fluffy fronds all over the place.

Growing conditions
Hare's foot likes lots of humidity and warmth. He would normally grow around the base of forest giants and loves decomposing leaf litter, so use a compost or potting mix with a high percentage of organic matter. It's important to keep moisture available around the roots without letting water sit around them. Coir is great for this because it holds onto water and releases it slowly to the roots.

Water and food
Soak the whole kokedama regularly to keep the soil moist, however let the ball dry out slightly before soaking again. Instead of overwatering by too much soaking, use a daily misting regime to keep his leaves happy. If a mister is nearby, it's easy to give him a spritz each time you pass by. Use a half-strength organic liquid fertilizer such as a seaweed-based option. Feed regularly in summer, usually once a month. Reduce in winter to avoid root burn. Apply a foliar feed a couple of times over his growth season but not in winter. This just gets added to his mister and applied directly to his leaves.

TREES AND
SHRUBS

Environment and care

Normally trees would grow outside, fully exposed to the elements. Be cautious when choosing trees to keep indoors. Fruiting plants need their flowers to be pollinated in order to produce fruit. This means that insects must have access to the flowers for that portion of the year when the tree is in bloom. Fruiting trees will need to spend several weeks each year outside. Consider this commitment when imagining how amazing a lemon tree will look in your kitchen window. Many trees are deciduous. Their leaves drop in the winter. Be prepared for this to happen if you think an acer will look great in your airy lounge (living room). Will the lounge (living room) look great with leaves all over the floor and do you have the styling finesse required to pull off a naked tree indoors?

IN A KOKEDAMA?

Because of the nature of their roots, as a general rule, trees will not become much larger than the size when you first make them up into a kokedama. Because trees have so many leaves and have a very active transpiration cycle (water loss through pores in the leaves), they have heavy water requirements. Make the ball as large as possible and use as much moss as you can. The soil recipes in general are acidic and rich in organic matter. Trees depend on the microprocesses which happen with the breakdown of matter to get the micronutrients they need to flourish. They will stay alive without access to these but will be much more susceptible to disease and infection and less healthy overall.

RECOMMENDED ROOM

Trees in general have very high light requirements and prefer several hours of direct sunlight each day. Unless you can source a tree which is specifically shade-loving, only the brightest room will be sufficient. Even then most homes would not normally have the height needed to accommodate a large tree, or the windows required to provide adequate light.

RECOMMENDED WATERING METHOD

If trees are too big and cumbersome, water them by placing a flexitub or large bucket up under the ball to be held in place with a stool. Once in place the bucket can be filled and the ball will soak up the water. When sufficient water has been taken up into the ball, remove the stool but leave the bucket under the ball to catch any drips. Regular misting will help alleviate dust build-up on the leaves. Trees will appreciate a good wash down occasionally, either in the shower with tepid water or outside under a hose.

Add a good quality organic liquid fertilizer to the water bucket once a month during summer, but not in winter.

Opposite: Organic liquid fertilizer is added to the soaking bucket of an olive tree

Tree kokedama

Large trees are definitely for the advanced kokedama maker. The process requires careful planning and high levels of dexterity.

Use a synthetic twine or string to prevent ball collapse.

Start by cutting 4 equal lengths of twine approximately 2 metres (7 feet) in length. Tie all 4 pieces together in the centre of the lengths. Place the knot on the ground and fan the ends out into a circle. Place a large sheet of coconut fibre matting (used to line hanging baskets) on top of the knot and cover with saturated sphagnum moss. Remove the tree from the pot and carefully loosen roots. Be careful not to damage any new root growth as this could result in the tree getting root shock.

Right: A swamp maple is being readied for transforming into a kokedama

1. Once the tree is in place, pile the soil recipe around the root ball. Cover top of root ball and soil mixture with moss. Pat down firmly to make it all stick together and stay on the ball.

2. Continue to cover the ball with moss until it reaches the underneath layer of moss. Cover top of ball and moss with more pieces of coconut fibre matting until you have enough that the 2 halves will meet when tied up.

3. Take a pair of the ends of twine or string you fanned out on the ground at the start and tie them together. This is the part which seems simple but is actually alike to a circus trick. You need to use the fibre matting to hold all the guts together.

4. Repeat with the remaining pairs of string ends. Trim the excess or tie them around again if long enough. Use your roll of twine to wrap the ball in an evenly random pattern until the ball is firm and secure. Cut off twine and poke end into ball.

Acer palmatum
Japanese maple

Family name
Sapindaceae

Type
Deciduous tree

Light
Full sun

Watering
High

Growth speed
Very slow

Pets
Pet friendly

Common concerns
Overwatering, underwatering

SOIL RECIPE
2 parts compost
4 parts coir
1 portion water crystals

Found in gardens around the globe, maple trees are hard to beat for drama. Attractive leaf shapes and spectacular displays of colour provide something truly unique. Japanese maples are typically found in sheltered gardens. There are numerous options within the species.

Acer is stunning as an indoor specimen, providing something completely unexpected. During the spring he will put on an intriguing display of new life as leaf buds emerge. Summer brings a rippling mane of verdant green or purple leaves. Autumn (fall) brings a blush of orange followed by pinks and reds. When dormant during winter, the tree's delicate bones are shown in an elegant repose.

Growing conditions
As a tree accustomed to growing outside in full exposure to all the elements, make sure he is in a position inside which will be acceptable to him. Light is the biggest concern. He really needs 6 to 8 hours of sunlight each day during summer. With this in mind only high ceilinged rooms with windows on 2 or 3 sides, or rooms with large skylights will be adequate. Alternatively, he is more than happy to live outside on a porch or hanging outside a window, but protect him from frost.

Water and food
During spring, when your acer is growing all his new clothes, he will need plenty of water to make them. He will also require plenty of food during this period. Once all his leaves are grown and luscious, he will need plenty of water to replace what is lost each day through transpiration (water vapour escaping through pores in the leaves). Don't let him dry out or he could lose his leaves prematurely. In the wild he would not typically be exposed to drought conditions. When his leaves start to turn for autumn (fall), begin reducing the food and water provided. Once all his leaves are gone, he doesn't require any food or water, but should not be allowed to completely dry out.

Citrus x limon 'Meyer'
Meyer's lemon

Family name
Rutaceae

Type
Fruiting evergreen tree

Light
Full sun

Watering
Moderate to high

Growth speed
Slow

Pets
Pet friendly

Common concerns
Root rot, collar rot, viral diseases,
pest invasions

SOIL RECIPE
3 parts compost
1 part coir
2 parts potting mix
1 part perlite
1 portion water crystals
1 portion slow-release
   organic fertilizer

While often cultivated for their fruit in backyards all over the world, lemons are actually a stunning tree to look at all the time. They have glossy dark green fragrant leaves and are evergreen, so always look lush. Lemons are great for suspended kokedama because they don't like being cold and they love humidity around their roots, not sitting water though as this will lead to root rot. They are fruit-bearing so they will need to be outside for the duration of their flowering period in order for the flowers to be pollinated. Leaving a window wide open may be sufficient. If you are really keen you can hand-pollinate. There are other books dedicated to that particular art form.

Growing conditions
He likes well-drained, nitrogen-rich, slightly acidic soil so make sure the compost and potting mix used are citrus specific. Normally grafted to a rootstock of a different variety, make sure the graft union is well out of the ball to avoid collar rot. The addition of a small amount of perlite will ensure there is still drainage through the ball to alleviate the common root rot problem of waterlogged citrus. Suspension also helps to prevent the build-up of residual water for gross stuff to grow in. The additional airflow helps to keep the whole situation much cleaner and fresher.

Water and food
Apart from during his growth period in spring, lemon needs the same amount of water all year round. Only allow the ball to dry on the surface before soaking again. His roots are slow-growing so it's best to reinforce your wrapping with a layer of synthetic twine or fishing nylon. He will need a nitrogen-rich fertilizer such as fish- or seaweed-based products. He can also get a magnesium deficiency which manifests as yellowing leaves. Add a little Epsom salts to his water occasionally to prevent this. He will need additional water and food while he is growing fruit – lack of water will stunt the growth of fruit, which will grow to normal size if enough water is provided.

Corokia cotoneaster
Wire-netting bush

Family name
Argophyllaceae

Type
Hardy evergreen shrub

Light
Bright

Watering
Moderate to high

Growth speed
Slow

Pets
Pet friendly

Common concern
Overwatering

SOIL RECIPE
2 parts compost
2 parts coir
2 parts potting mix
1 part perlite

Although corokia is widely grown in the northern hemisphere, he is native to New Zealand. He will grow to be a dense and gnarly shrub in the wild but will become dwarfed when in a kokedama and stay about the same size as when created. The lovely fine branches are covered with many tiny dark green leaflets. Corokia are great for bringing delicate interest to close spaces which would be crowded or overwhelmed by leafy lush plants. It is possible to find very small seedlings which will become thicker in the trunk and may produce new branches but will ultimately stay very petite. These guys are perfect for bright corners or sunny terraces, adding screening without blocking too much of the light. They look amazing suspended in a corner window; they throw strong shadows into the room through all their twisty branches. The corokia is evergreen so he keeps his leaves during winter. He will drop his old leaves all through the year – a normal process for evergreen trees and shrubs.

Growing conditions
Requiring either full sun or only partial shade, the corokia is an ideal candidate for a lovely sunny conservatory. He will be okay in a room which only gets direct sun for half the day but would prefer up to 8 hours of direct sun during the summer. He is a shrub and expects all the extremities of a temperate climate. He may get confused about when to produce his little yellow flowers if he doesn't get winter chilling and summer cooking. For best results he would enjoy a midseason vacation to an outdoor setting for up to 4 weeks in both summer and winter (but avoid frost).

Water and food
Corokia only has tiny wee leaves but when he has lots of them, they use a lot of water. In summer, allow the ball to dry on the surface before soaking again. In the winter, it's okay to let him dry out a bit more as he will have fewer leaves and require less moisture. His roots are slow-growing so it's best to reinforce your wrapping with a layer of synthetic twine or fishing nylon.

Olea europaea
Olive

Family name
Oleaceae

Type
Evergreen fruiting tree

Light
Full sun

Watering
Moderate to high

Growth speed
Slow

Pets
Pet friendly

Common concern
Tricky to fruit indoors

SOIL RECIPE
2 parts compost
1 part coir
3 parts potting mix
1 portion water crystals
1 portion slow-release
   organic fertilizer

The ancestry of the olive is not known for sure, but it has been a staple of the Mediterranean since ancient times. Although there are about 30 species of olive, by far the most common is *Olea europaea*. The many cultivars within this species are grown for their variously flavoured fruits. Leathery, dusky, grey-green leaves touched with silver on the underside, paired with a languid and luxurious growing habit, make him hard to beat when accenting a clean white space. His soft grey bark adds to the perfection of his understated tones. Use a natural coloured twine or a clear fishing nylon to wrap so as not to detract from the muted misty beauty.

Growing conditions
Although olives are very tolerant trees that often grow well in poor soil, they won't complain about having nice soil to grow in. The tricky thing about indoor olive trees is getting them to fruit. The tree itself will thrive in a lovely warm and dry home, but in order to fruit he needs to be chilled sufficiently in winter and needs to be exposed to long hot days during the summer. A winter vacation to the outdoors for a few weeks, as long as he doesn't get frosted, should do the trick for winter chilling so flowers will set. In order to get the fruit to mature and ripen, though, he really needs 8 or more hours of direct sunlight each day. Considering that the size of the crop one could yield from a single indoor olive tree would be handfuls at the most, it's probably not worth the effort – but he is stunning just as a foliage tree.

Water and food
Soak the kokedama when the ball is almost completely dry. Do not overwater. He likes arid and barren land, so too much water will just rot his roots. He will need a light feed each season to keep him healthy. Use a good organic liquid fertilizer at half strength added to his water 4 times a year.

HERBS

Environment and care

Herbs are tricky because they are such a broad group of plants. For the sake of simplicity, only shrubby culinary plants have been selected for inclusion. The possibilities for incorporating these amazing plants into a home via kokedama are vast. The main factor to consider is that the light and water requirement for some herbs, such as basil, will be prohibitive when choosing a candidate for kokedama. Stay with the woody stemmed perennial herbs which will stick around for more than a few weeks. Herbs with rapid lush growth will be too demanding to be worthwhile in a kokedama.

Left: Large herb gardens are too cumbersome to soak frequently – water from above instead

Above: Herbs require plenty of light – if indoors is not proving light enough, move your kokedama to a sunny outdoor spot

IN A KOKEDAMA?

Because herbs are intrinsically cropping plants, as in they produce a crop, they need to be treated as such. They will need lots of food in the form of sunshine as well as organic fertilizer. Remember you can only get out what you put in. If you intend to pick your herbs for use in the kitchen you will need to keep a close eye on them to make sure they don't become malnourished. Keep a good quality organic fertilizer in liquid form handy and give small amounts regularly at half strength.

RECOMMENDED ROOM

For herbs to remain viable they ideally need 8 hours of full sunlight each day. They rely on sunlight to produce new growth; a lack of sunlight will lead to leggy, weak plants. Keep them hanging outside the kitchen window where they can be easily watered and tended as well as picked. If the kitchen window isn't an option then hang inside a patio area or from the eaves of the sunniest side of the building. The only way herbs would get enough light inside is if they were in a corner window facing the sunrise, or in a window which also had a skylight above it.

RECOMMENDED WATERING METHOD

Because of the open neck of the ball it is easy to top-water. Simply pour water into the top of the ball until it starts to drip. This needs to be done frequently enough that the herb plant doesn't experience any root drying. If his roots get dry he might think there is a drought and burst into flower, then die. Hardy perennials don't tend to be as dramatic and are a little more tolerant of dry balls, but still err on the side of too much rather than too little water. Drought conditions can lead to bitter herbs.

133

Herb garden kokedama

For this project 3 plants are incorporated into one kokedama to create a hanging herb garden. It is critical to select herbs that will live happily together. A simple solution is to choose 3 similar herbs from within the same family. They will need to share the same basic soil and environmental requirements. Many herbs are available in decorative variants, such as variegated oregano, which will add visual interest to your creation. Alternatively have a chat with the expert at your local garden centre and they should be able to recommend plants which will do well together in your area.

Remove all plants from their pots and loosen soil.

Gently but firmly tie all 3 plant root balls together. You want them to be secure enough to handle as one unit.

Don't tie the string so tight as to damage any of the fragile roots, though. Young herbs generally have very tender roots and will often sulk if over-handled.

From this point on you can follow the wrapping directions at the front of the book and treat your clump of plants as one.

By necessity the ball will be significantly larger than what you would normally make. Especially consider that you want to provide enough nutrients for the plants to produce edible quantities of leaves. Use a generous amount of soil mixture.

Because there are 3 separate plants competing for moisture and food, you will have to account for this in the initial design. The ball will probably end up with quite a large neck opening, which in this case makes watering from above very practical.

Use a really thick layer of moss to protect the soil inside from moisture loss by evaporation. If you have a particularly dry home you can add a layer of coconut fibre to the outside as well.

Left: Herbs are removed from pots and tied together; the group of plants can now be treated as a single unit

Opposite: A herb garden kokedama using thyme, marjoram and variegated oregano

Origanum vulgare
Oregano

Family name
Lamiaceae

Type
Aromatic perennial

Light
Bright

Watering
Moderate

Growth speed
Moderate

Pets
Pet friendly

Common concern
Malnutrition

SOIL RECIPE
1 part compost
2 parts potting mix
2 parts coir
1 part perlite

Oregano is a member of the mint family so he enjoys hot sunny conditions. Also known as wild marjoram, he is a bushy creeping ground cover. When you put him in a kokedama, he will make lovely trails and falls of leaves over the edge of his ball. He doesn't mind the occasional dry spell and hates having soggy roots. He is an ideal candidate for hanging in a sunny kitchen window where you can pick a few leaves to add to your pizza.

Growing conditions
He grows best if given bright or full sun for most of the day. He doesn't like overly rich soil, which is why there is coir in his mix. He doesn't like his roots to get soggy so we add perlite into his mixture to help the water drain through the ball and not sit around getting stale.

Water and food
He doesn't actually consume that much water and will be much happier about morning misting rather than too frequent soaking of his ball. Soak him when the ball is dry to the touch but allow to dry more between watering during winter. During spring, he will need a half-strength dose of food every 2 weeks to keep him lush. Don't feed over winter. Use a good quality organic liquid fertilizer.

Rosmarinus officinalis
Rosemary

Family name
Lamiaceae

Type
Aromatic evergreen shrub

Light
Bright

Watering
Moderate

Growth speed
Moderate

Pets
Pet friendly

Common concern
Malnutrition

SOIL RECIPE
3 parts compost
2 parts potting mix
2 parts coir
1 part perlite

Rosemary has the scraggy beauty of a wild pixie child. He has lovely curly, twisty, adventurous branches covered all over with tiny dark green leaflets. He will flower in the spring if he has a period of cooler temperatures over winter. He produces masses of tiny flowers all over his stems. Ranging from white through pink to blues, they can be quite a show if you can get him to flower indoors. A winter vacation outdoors for a couple of weeks may help to set flowers for spring. Woody stems mean he can hold crazy poses and make brilliant shapes without wearing himself out. New growth emerges as velveteen white stems with crisp forest green leaflets.

Growing conditions
He grows best if given bright or full sun for most of the day. A sunny kitchen window is perfect for your rosemary. Although much hardier than one would expect of such a useful herb, and chilling is often required to set flowers, he won't enjoy being completely frozen. Protect from harsh frosts by hanging up high under cover, such as under the eaves of a roof, while on winter sojourns to the outdoors.

Water and food
He likes humidity around his roots during the hot summer, so water him when the ball is dry to the touch but not completely so during summer. Allow to dry almost completely between watering during winter. The biggest problem with rosemary in a kokedama is that he is a hungry little guy so during spring he will need a half-strength dose of food every 2 weeks to keep him lush. Don't feed over winter. Use a good quality organic liquid fertilizer.

Thymus vulgaris Common thyme

Family name
Lamiaceae

Type
Aromatic dwarf shrub

Light
Bright

Watering
Moderate

Growth speed
Moderate

Pets
Pet friendly

Common concern
Malnutrition

SOIL RECIPE
1 part compost
2 parts potting mix
2 parts coir
1 part perlite

Thyme is a woody creeping evergreen ground cover in the wild. He has lovely grey-green leaves which are highly aromatic. Just like oregano, he is a member of the mint family and hails from the Mediterranean so doesn't mind the occasional dry spell. He will be a great window companion for oregano, as they are cousins, and not only enjoy hanging out together but when combined in cooking add a lovely depth of flavour.

Growing conditions
Like oregano, thyme, too, grows best if given bright or full sun for most of the day. He prefers well drained soil that isn't too rich in organic matter. He is a cropping plant so won't appreciate completely barren conditions. Adding perlite to the potting mix helps water to drain through the ball. Adding compost will give him the food he needs.

Water and food
In the wild he would grow on the hot and parched lands of southern Europe. He is accustomed to long periods of dry conditions. He won't mind regular watering but if he becomes too soggy his roots will start to rot. Mimic dew fall with regular morning misting. Soak him when the ball is dry to the touch. Allow him to dry more between watering during winter, when he is less active. During spring he will need a half-strength dose of food every 2 weeks to keep him lush. Use a good quality organic liquid fertilizer.

Suppliers and definitions

SUPPLIERS

United Kingdom

CROCUS
www.crocus.co.uk
Biggest online resource for
gardening supplies in the UK.
Plants, tools and materials.

DOTTED LINE WORKSHOPS
www.dottedlineworkshops.com
London-based provider of
unique workshops. Offers regular
kokedama classes and supplies.

HIGHGROVE GARDENS
www.highgrovegardens.com
The private gardens of Their Royal
Highnesses The Prince of Wales
and The Duchess of Cornwall.
Plants, seeds, twine and tools.

LONGACRES
www.longacres.co.uk
Longacres Garden Centre is
a premier source of gardening
supplies in the UK. Plants, twine
fertilizer, tools and accessories.

NUTSCENE
nutscene.com
Jute twines in beautiful colours.

RAREPLANTS
www.rareplants.co.uk
New, rare and noteworthy plants
not found in your local garden
centre. Specializes in rare and
unusual species bulbs.

ROWAN GARDEN CENTRE
www.rowangardencentre.co.uk
A wide variety of plants and lots
of other stuff too — pots, tools
and much more.

THE JAPAN SOCIETY
www.japansociety.org.uk
Enhancing the British-Japanese
relationship in the UK. Provides
workshops on kokedama.

TRANQUIL PLANTS
www.tranquilplants.co.uk
Online supplier of kokedama
and workshops.

TRIANGLE NURSERY
www.trianglenursery.co.uk
Wholesale floristry supplies. Wide
selection of moss in different
varieties, colours and sizes.

TWOOL
shop.twool.co.uk
British wool alternative to imported
jute. A wide range of twine and
gardening tools.

United States

AMAZON
www.amazon.com
Amazon is an online repository of
all the things you could ever want,
including plant misters, twine,
scissors, and tools.

JOSH'S FROGS
www.joshsfrogs.com
Frog breeders, related supplies.
Stocks the same long-stranded
moss supplied from the same
farms as used in the book.

PISTILS NURSERY
shop.pistilsnursery.com
This store in Portland, Oregon,
was founded in 2001 as a haven
for plant lovers. Sells kokedama,
plants and runs kokedama
workshops.

REPOTME.COM
www.repotme.com
Orchid, bonsai and gardening
supplies. Moss, media, materials,
tools and sundries.

ZOO MED
zoomed.com
Online store stocking a wide range
of terrarium supplies including live
decorative moss.

New Zealand

BATH BOUTIQUE
www.bathboutique.co.nz
Kokedama and twine.

PAPER PLANE STORE
www.paperplanestore.com
All tools and equipment which
appear in this book were

generously supplied by Paper Plane Store. Ceramics are available from Paper Plane.

PICKLED WHIMSY
www.pickledwhimsy.co.nz
Home to kokedama, twine, moss and Coraleigh Alice ceramics.

Australia

AUSTRALIAN ORCHID NURSERY
www.australianorchids.com.au
Wide range of moss; live sphagnum, live fancy, dyed and dried.

LIVING ARTE
www.livingarte.com.au
Melbourne-based studio selling kokedama.

Europe

BAKKER
www.bakker.com
Online garden supply website shipping to all of Europe. Plants, gardening supplies and materials.

KOKEDAMA ARTE
www.art-du-kokedama.fr
Online store based in France. Kokedama supplies, kokedama and workshops.

LUCKY REPTILE
www.luckyreptile.com
Germany-based terrarium and reptile supplier. Sells the same New Zealand moss as used throughout the book.

WE SMELL THE RAIN
wesmelltherain.com
Amsterdam-based company creating beautiful ways to bring nature indoors. Kokedama, hanging options, accessories.

DEFINITIONS

akadama: clay granules from Japan, used in the traditional form of kokedama

epiphyte: tropical plants, often with aerial roots, found growing on tree trunks rather than in the ground

kokedama: a living art form that displays a plant with its roots wrapped in a ball of soil and moss

misting: spraying a plant with fine water droplets as a boost to humidity

naturalization: the process by which a kokedama ball is gradually colonized on the outside by moss and held together inside by its own roots

nearai: this style of bonsai, where the plants have no pots, gave rise to kokedama

transpiration: water lost as vapour through tiny pores in a leaf's surface

wabi-sabi: Japanese philosophy that finds beauty in imperfection and embraces transience

wrapping style: the look created by the choice of string and pattern formed by looping it over the moss ball

Acknowledgements

The biggest thanks have to go to Larnie Nicolson. What an amazing talent and an astoundingly amazing human. So much empathy and love for the world. Absolutely endless patience and calm (when many would have totally lost their minds!) I am in complete awe of your talent, Larnie, you truly are one of the greats. I feel privileged to have worked with you so closely for such a lot of your time. Without you this book would not exist. Thank you times a million.

Haley Ashby, for being the most amazing human ever. Without you, Haley, I would not be where I am. You started it all by inviting me to share your stand with you at our local market. You have encouraged and supported me through every trial and celebrated every success. I wish there was a more fitting way to express my gratitude. These words seem pale compared to what you contribute to the world. I know I am not the only one who has benefited from having your light shined on them.

Adam, for patiently accepting all the drama. For the late night stress sessions, for the meltdowns and the breakdowns. For the spell checks and raised eyebrows. You're my everything. Thank you for letting me be me, and for delighting in it.

To my mum, Helen, for all the plants. So many plants. For all your hours spent slaving away in my nursery making plant babies and making sure the watering got done. For gardening with me at your feet as a tiny child and letting me explore my curiosity (eating snails) instead of crushing it.

To my dad, David, even though I know I really stretch your ability to support me with my crazy ideas – thanks for continuing on regardless. For the impromptu builds and last-minute frantic preparations and the many, many iterations of ideas. For acknowledging that I struggle to fit into boxes provided by society; thanks for noticing and thanks for not trying to force me.

Felicity Mitchel, you are so talented and beautiful. You inspire me. I aspire to be as effortlessly elegant and put together as you. Additionally, as a side note: thank you for being a Good Grammar Advocate when I had reached my limit. Your passion helped get me back on track and finish what seemed like an impossible task.

Krista Plews, you are the pinnacle of flawless design. I cannot convey my gratitude to you with words which would be adequate to the contribution you have made to me as a creative. You have supported and calmly guided me towards making a product that is truly and simply beautiful. Without your careful and relentless editing of my work, it would not be what it is today. Thank you for believing in me and sticking with me while I got it right.

Denise Moore, you are a saint. Thank you for looking after the kids without question or bother whenever we asked. I truly appreciate that you have just as much going on in your super busy life. Thank you for giving me the space to write when I needed it.

Therese Wally, hand model extraordinaire, all around good egg and pretty much the best assistant ever.

Nadine Thomas, what a legend. How did I end up all these years later with you doing handiwork for my book?!

Anouk Treutiger, for letting us into your home.

Hayley French @mylittlehouse, for allowing us to use your stunning home.

The Fitzsimmons family for letting us put moss everywhere and for the scrumptious smoothies!

Amanda Fitzsimmons @rococo_and_rose, your artwork is amazing!

Dion and Irene, for letting us into the best kept 70s secret in Ponsonby.

Leanne Martell, you are the nicest person ever. Thank you for being such a dream. Thank you for being so understanding of the challenging process of running a business and writing a book simultaneously.